Mal'akhim

Divine Intervention in One's Life

Mal'akhim

Divine Intervention in One's Life

Dr. Patania L. Eiland

Studio of Books LLC
5900 Balcones Drive Suite 100
Austin, Texas 78731
www.studioofbooks.org
Hotline: (254) 800-1183

Ordering Information:
Special discounts are available on quantity purchases by corporations, associations, and others. For details, contact the publisher at the address above.

Printed in the United States of America.

ISBN-13: Softcover 978-1-970283-76-1
Ebook 978-1-970283-77-8

Mal'akhim

"A story of the omnipresence of God Jehovah in one's life."

Table of Contents

God's Divine Messengers God's Divine Protectors

We are often told stories regarding Angels and that we all have a Guardian Angel. I remember, as a child, seeing a picture of two children walking across a tattered bridge, with an Angel standing behind them, guarding them as a shadow of protection. I believe as the Bible tells us in Psalms 91:11-12, ***"For He shall give His angels charge over you, to keep you in all your ways. In their hands they shall bear you up, lest you dash your foot against a stone"*** that Angels do exist and are either fighting for us and yes, unfortunately there is a fallen group of angels fighting against us. The truth be told, this fallen group, as enemies of God, are fighting against Him by either using us, or infiltrating hardships in our lives to taunt our God who loves and cares for each of us dearly.

Mal'ak is the Hebrew word for Angel. Mal'akhim is the plural for Angels. God uses His angels as messengers, guardians, and protectors for humankind. They can appear in many forms, from radiant rays of light to just a presence in the room. They can also take on human form. They can just speak in a soft voice or even a gentle touch. We are surrounded by them, whether we are attuned to their presence or not. They are right there with you right now as you read this book. Angels are watching over you. Every step you take and every move you make, their private eyes are watching you.

I believe that I have experienced angels holding me in a loving caress when I was in despair at a moment in my life. I have heard sweet whispers in my ear and have been awakened out of a deep sleep with a nudge on the shoulder to wake up. I do know that, as a 4-year-old, I believed I saw an angel in the basement of my dad's church, Springfield Missionary Baptist Church, in Cleveland, Ohio. Ever since that time, I have always believed in angels. When I got older and returned to the church, I realized that what I thought I saw wasn't an angel but a stain on the furnace. However, that did not change my belief that angels do exist and are real and imminent in our lives, and working in the backdrop of our lives. We may notice it, and may not notice, or should I say, there is a side of us that notices, but fears to acknowledge it.

We have to acknowledge that not all angels are good angels. We know that one of God's most beautiful angels rebelled against His Creator and led a third of the angelic realm to follow him. I believe that these, too, are at work. Whenever we are influenced or nudged to do wrong, it is not angels but imps that are the nucleus behind every bad thought and deed that makes us choose something other than God. When we choose to follow this group, we assist in the rebellion against God, our Creator. And as the Bible tells us, there is a specific place of damnation for these angels and all the humans that follow their lead of deception and evil doings. Hades.

This story tells of the journey of Olivia Hill, who has had a series of angels watching over her since birth. She has also dealt with the other beings that are called impulas and their evil forces and influences. However, throughout Olivia's life, not only have her assigned angels watched over her, but they have also befriended her and guided her to her 100th birthday. As she celebrates her 100th birthday, she is visited by her Angelic Friends, and they take Marlon Lamont, her grandson, who has a strong spiritual gift to see the good and the bad influences in people, and the Messengers of God and the fallen group on a journey to help him to understand not only the gift he has but also the journey of life with Mal'akhim guidance's and protection.

I want you to read and be blessed. But not only that, I want you to read and be observant of your own life journey. Ask yourself, have I encountered a Mal'ak? Have I been protected in some way that I know it had to be an angel? We never know when we are entertaining these Heavenly Beings. That is why it is vital that we treat every person we encounter with love and respect.

You never know when you are in the midst of a Mal'ak, a Divine Messenger, a Divine Protector.

Mal'akhim Divine Intervention in One's Life.

Be blessed!

And Happy Angelic reading.....

Dr. Patania L. Eiland

ALPHA

It was a beautiful day when the Walker family went out to the park. The sun was at its best, and the wind was just right with the breeze. Pretty blue skies with puffy, crystal-white clouds hanging sporadically made a beautiful picture. Ellen Walker thought, "What a wonderful God we serve to create such vast beauty. How we take it for granted—the sun's heat, the wind's breeze, and the birds and trees—all of God's beauty we engulf daily and sometimes without a "Thank You." The Walker family was a devout Christian family. Eddie Eugene Walker, pastor of a local congregation, and Ellen Walker, the most supportive 1st Lady, stood by his side and would be the first to say, "Preach Rev," whenever he delivered one of his powerful Sunday morning sermons. They had tried for years to have children, but due to medical issues that Ellen had with her heart, the doctor encouraged them not to try. After four miscarriages and many years of tears, God blessed them with a little girl they named Olivia. She weighed 6 pounds and 6 ounces, and her skin was a red nutmeg color; she looked almost angelic. She had beautiful black curly hair on nutmeg-red skin and big brown eyes that looked like Heaven when she looked up in your arms. Olivia was their pride and joy. They had spent this day together—a well-deserved time out from their busy church work. Rev. Walker had been promising for weeks to spend time with the family. The church business and pastoral care prevented him from doing so. So, that day was the one he set aside to share time with his family. It was getting dark, and they had at least a good hour to drive. The park was along a dark street with very few street lights, and they wanted to get going before dark hit them. However, the time spent was so enjoyable that they lost track of time and drove in the dark at night. About thirty minutes into the drive, Olivia began to cry; she needed her diaper changed. Ellen was trying to console the baby girl as

Eddie turned to look back to make Olivia smile. He took his eyes off the road for just a second, but when he looked back, there was a deer family consisting of a buck, a female deer, and a baby fawn crossing the road. It was too late for Eddie to steer the car to miss them, and he hit the buck and deer, veered off the road, and crashed into the tree. When Ellen had just a little conscience to sense what had happened, she could plainly see that Eddie was gone, and she knew that the injury she suffered was too severe for her to make it. She looked up to Heaven and prayed to God that He would send angels to care for baby Olivia, and as she prayed, she looked across the road and saw that both the buck and the mother deer were down, and the baby fawn was weeping over them, just as she could hear baby Olivia crying. Ellen prayed, "Please let my little girl live to be 100 years old." Then, all of a sudden, 7 brightly lit beams came down from the sky and stood around the baby fawn. Ellen prayed and said, "Thank You, Lord God Almighty," and took her last breath.

A story written by:

Rev. Patania L. Eiland

Please read the entire 7-volume copy and the Alpha and Omega parts to receive the full meaning and inspiration behind the book series "Mal'akhim."

This series of books is for children and those adults who have a childlike heart and can still imagine with a pure heart!

Read and be blessed!

CHAPTER I

Meet Jeremiah "The Beginning of Divine Intervention."

"Olivia Hill is my name," she said to the doctor as she lay in her hospital bed. "My name is Olivia Hill, and I am 100 years old today." She coughed and gasped for breath. "I have lived a long and beautiful life and an adventurous one, too. So you see, Dr. Davis, I'm not afraid of dying." She was right; she had lived a beautiful life that was more than adventurous but filled with close calls, breakthroughs, and divine interventions. Now, she lay in her bed, feeble and stricken but still in good spirits. Olivia still looked good for her age. She stood five feet tall with beautiful nutmeg skin that was still as smooth as a baby's bottom. Her long, beautiful white hair was the only thing that gave her age away. "Guess what? I'm 100 years old and still have all my teeth," she said, smiling and showing them to the doctor. Dr. Michael Artis Davis had been her physician for the past 40 years. He was still young, in his late 60s. "I have to ask you this question just to see if you remember," he said. "Oh, I remember when you first became a doctor," she said strongly, "27 years old. You were so young; remember what I told you when we met?" "I do," he said in his calm, still voice as he checked her vision. "However, that wasn't the first time we met," he said under his breath. He smiled, saying, "You told me that you weren't a Barbie doll or GI Joe toy and that you were made of flesh and had a soul." They both laughed. "Yeah, and I remember your response. You said, "Well, let's just stick you with this needle and see." She laughed with a hard cough. "Easy now," said Dr. Davis, gently touching her back. "I knew then that you were a good doctor because you had a sense of humor." Olivia was always laughing and enjoying life to its fullest. She had a way of making the best of every situation. She was a devout Christian, believing God would always see her through. "You can always tell a good doctor by their bedside manners," she said as she sipped a drink of her water. "You know, you don't look like you've aged a bit," she said as she leaned up from her bed. “Lie down and get your rest, my dear,” he said again in a still calm voice. “In fact, the more I look at you, the more I see that you really don’t look too much different from the doctor I had when I was a little girl. Now, he was an exceptional doctor; he would play with me and give me candy every time I visited.” “It was a Blow Pop, cherry-flavored,” Dr. Davis said. “Yes, how did you know?” Olivia looked at him with amazement, and the more she did, the more he reminded her of Dr. Williams. “Perhaps because you’ve told me this story many times,” he said with a smile.” Now lie down and don’t excite yourself. You will soon have visitors coming to see you, and you want to be well-rested,” said Dr. Davis as he left the room and smiled. Olivia couldn’t sleep because she knew she had never told him that story before. She thought to herself, “I know I’m old and somewhat sickly, but I am in my right frame of mind, and I know that I’ve never told him that story before, because it was just now that he reminded me of Dr. Williams.” Olivia had been a sickly child; in fact, the doctors told her foster parents that she wouldn’t live past five years old and said that if she lived, her life would be limited due to her heart condition. She had a weak heart when she was born. Just like her mom. She was a premature baby, and back then, medical inventions were not as advanced. But she remembered that her foster mother told her that her mom had prayed to God to take care of her child, bless her, and send her healing from above. Olivia was born to the Reverend Eddie Eugene Walker and Ellen Olivia Walker. Yes, she had her mother's middle name. They were her biological parents, who died in a car accident when Olivia was just a baby. Before her mother took her last breath, she asked God to send his angels to care for baby Olivia. Her foster parents were strong believers in God, and they raised her to be a godly woman. As a matter of fact, her foster mother and father, Rev. James Dan Love and Mrs. Bertha Love, would be considered agents of God to care for the baby girl. Through them and even the friends she encountered and met along the way, you would say they were divine assets. And here she rested in a hospital bed in her dying hours. God certainly kept His promise to Olivia's mother 100 years ago. Olivia was lying there thinking about her life, and she shouted with holy laughter and said aloud in an emotional hallelujah voice," Thank You, God," as tears rolled from her eyes of gratitude. Her shout was so loud that it aroused the entire hospital floor. The charge nurse, Merle, came running in and asked frantically, "Are you alright, Ms. Olivia?" She said as she wept in a quivering voice, "Yes, God has been really good to me, and I just had to thank Him."

Merle said, "He sure has. You are still here; I hope I live to see as many years as you have and beat all the odds you have overcome, Ms. Olivia." Olivia looked at Merle and said, "Child, how long have you been working here?" "Oh, for a good while," Merle said as she dimmed the lights. "Get some rest now; you will have visitors coming soon." Olivia looked at her and said, "I know you've been working here for a while; in fact, you look like the nurse I had when I was a child; you are just a little less hippy than she was, but child, when I look at your face, it is the same face. Was your mother a nurse, too?" Merle touched her on the shoulder and said in the sweetest voice, "Rest now," and walked out the door. This puzzled Olivia seriously because, when she began to reflect on her life, both Merle and Dr. Davis looked like the same people who cared for her years ago and had the same mannerisms. In fact, the nurse, when she was a child, would touch her on the shoulder, just as Merle did, and say the same thing. Olivia thought about it, then said, "Maybe it's the new medication they are giving me. I must be hallucinating or something, or I have the old people's disease of the mind." She laughed and said, "I am 100 years old," then drifted off to sleep.

As she was sleeping, one of her oldest and dearest friends, Jeremiah, visited her. Jeremiah was tall, strong, dark, and handsome. He had the thickest curly black hair, and his olive smooth skin tone and big baby blue eyes attracted Olivia to Jeremiah. Not only was he pleasant to look at, but he also had the kindest of hearts. He and Olivia had been friends since grade school. As Olivia lay sleeping, Jeremiah thought about when he first officially met Olivia. They were in kindergarten together. Yes, they were lifetime friends. Jeremiah had known Olivia all her life. Olivia had always been frail in stature and weak due to her health, even in kindergarten. There were bullies in the class. Yes, children can be cruel even at five years of age. There was a particular bully named Bossk. He was a chubby boy who looked like he should've been in the 6th grade. He liked to throw his weight around in kindergarten. Bossk would pick on Olivia because of her size and would make comments like "If I breathe on you, you would fall down" and "There isn't a word for someone skinnier than skinny." Olivia was very small for her age. The doctor told her foster mom to give her a piece of chocolate candy after each meal so that she would gain weight. Olivia thought it was great, and she would eat the miniature Mr. Goodbars and Hershey's chocolate bars after each meal as a treat. It was Jeremiah who put a stop to Bossk's mistreatments. As he sat there thinking about old times, Olivia moved and groaned. He touched her hand, and she said softly, "Jeremiah, I know it's you; I can tell by your touch and the sweet fragrance you have always worn. It reminds me of that holy oil Ms. Bertha would get from the Bible bookstore." Jeremiah spoke very quietly and said, "Yes, it is me. I came to check on you and see how you were doing." She said as she chuckled, "Old Jeremiah, always coming to my rescue. I know if you could, you would heal me with the snap of your finger." "Yes, I would, Olivia; I love you that much. Do you remember when we first met in kindergarten?" He asked, trying to keep her mind off the pain she was feeling as she squinted her eyes and pressed the pain button. She said, "Yes, Mrs. Burch's class." Jeremiah said, "Yes, Mrs. Burch's class. I don't know which is worse: being in her class or dealing with that big bully Bossk." "I would say Bossk; he was ornery and a mean little boy. I believe he was the devil himself," she said with a stronger voice. "Well, he wasn't the devil, but he had devilish tendencies," said Jeremiah. As they reminisced, both their minds went back to Beehive Elementary School. The halls were large, and even in grade school, the children had lockers, which was cool. The principal was Mrs. Greenly, who ruled the school like a military yard. She stood tall and heavy, and when she walked, it felt like the entire school was shaking. Everything behind her was as big as she was tall, and she had the thickest eyebrows, which looked like they were all in one line. Olivia laughed really hard as Jeremiah was telling the story. He said, "You laugh because she was especially nice to you, but the rest of us had no chance with Mrs. Greenly." "I laugh because I remember when Bossk got caught bringing a frog into the school, and Mrs. Greenly saw him. He wasn't so much a bully then. Mrs. Greenly stared him down, and with just that one look she gave him, Bossk went to the bathroom on himself. Do you remember that, Jeremiah?" "Oh yeah, I remember that day, and he smelled all day." "Yeah, and he didn't mess with me that day at all; in fact, he seemed to calm down quite a bit after that incident." Olivia was sitting up by this time, and she looked at her friend and said, "Jeremiah, when I really think about it, you have been a wonderful friend to me. It seems like every time I was in trouble, you were always there to either take up for me or get me out of a jam. Sometimes, I thought it was unseeingly strange how you would just show up at the right time." Jeremiah smiled and said in his deep, strong voice, "That's what friends are for. I wouldn't have it any other way."

"Olivia, do you remember when we were walking home from school along the railroad tracks, and there was a hidden cave we found?" Jeremiah leaned in close to her as he spoke softly. "I remember it well," Olivia said as her eyes widened with excitement. "Remember, I told you not to go in the cave, and for some reason, you just couldn't resist?" Olivia said, "I don't remember if it was me that wanted to go; I thought that Porchia and Lenny wanted to go in, and they dared us to go in." Jeremiah looked and said, "Yes, that was pure peer pressure." "I think it was easy for me because I had a crush on Lenny Maxwell,"

Olivia smiled as if she were looking at Lenny right then. "I thought he was the cutest," Olivia said with the biggest grin. "He had that pretty dark, smooth skin with those thick eyelashes. Oh, what I would give to have eyelashes like that! And to think that as a boy, even as a man, he still had them thick, long eyelashes. He was the cutest to me, aside from you, Jeremiah." Jeremiah said, "I know, but it's hard to believe we spent 4 hours in that cave." "Yeah, time flies when you are having fun," she said, with her pretty dark brown eyes growing. Oh, our parents were so angry with us. "It was all because you were following in behind Lenny," Jeremiah said as he pointed at her as if he was going to tickle her like he always did. "Lenny had the most pretty hazel-brown eyes," Olivia continued to reminisce. "Yes, Olivia, you had a weak spot for guys with different colored eyes," Jeremiah said with a sigh and rolled his eyes. "Yes, that's true. I believe that's why I fell in love with you," she said before she knew it. "In love?" Jeremiah asked as he looked at her with a surprised look. "Jeremiah, you know I love you and have always had a crush on you. I guess it's okay to tell you, even though I'm too old to do anything about it now." Jeremiah laughed with a thunder of laughter—the kind that makes you bend over and gasp for air. "Why are you laughing so hard? Jeremiah, I don't see anything funny. Oh, so you think that's funny?" Olivia was upset now. She said, "Just see if I tell you anything else. I'm mad now, Jeremiah." He finally caught his breath. He explained, "No, Olivia, I'm laughing because you fell in love with just about anybody who spent more than 2 minutes with you." "Oh, hush up, Jeremiah," she said, waving her hand at him to tell him to go away. "What are you trying to say about me, Jeremiah, that I'm some kind of floozy?" "No, dear, just that you have such a soft heart for everybody. I have to tell you that you have never met a stranger and have always cared for people more than normal. That's why I always had to get you out of situations. It was nearly always because you had let your heart fall for the wrong guy, or were nice to the wrong people who had bad intentions for you, or were just getting you out of a jam where you allowed someone to con you into something because you didn't know how to say no to people." "Really, Jeremiah, that's what you think about me?" "No, Olivia, that's what I know about you. It's okay; it doesn't make you a bad person at all; in fact, it shows how big your heart is, and that's a good thing," he said, as he leaned forward to kiss her on the forehead. "I don't remember a thing that you are talking about, Jeremiah," she said adamantly. "Well, let me remind you," he said.

"Just like the time when we wandered into the cave. I knew it was a bad idea, but you let Lenny and Porchia talk you into it. I told you, "No, we need to get home before dark." All it took was for Lenny to ask if you liked him, and that was it. That cave was dark and smelly, and I knew that it was a bad idea. There was a smell of some kind of chemical in the cave, and there were rats, spiders, and all kinds of creepy crawling things. Normally, you would notice them, but you were so engrossed with Lenny that you paid the big spider I pulled out of your hair no mind. Nor did you see the big puddle of mud you stepped into, nearly ruining your favorite blue suede shoes. It was Lenny,

Lenny, Lenny. That wasn't the only time you let Lenny get you into a fix." "That's all, Jeremiah. Is that all you have for me?" Olivia said as she turned her face to the wall to ignore him. "No," he said, as he

grabbed her chin, "I have plenty of examples of you allowing people to fool you or get you into a spot of bother." "Like what?" She said as she poked her lips out with a pout.

"For example, you always fell for Bossk's schemes, and I knew he was up to no good, but you, Olivia, just didn't see the bad in anyone. Like the day Bossk led you out to the cornfield once during recess.

"Come on, Olivia, I know you want to see the baby birds in the field. There is a nest out here," Bossk said as he was smirking under his breath. George Freeman and Danny Smith were always in the pack with Bossk. They were the most mischievous children anyone could ever meet. George was tall and skinny, with a long nose that always made him look like he was up to no good. And Danny, short and rugged but sneaky, would always throw spitballs and then act as if he didn't know what was happening. He would get away with it because he was so small. I couldn't believe you would fall for their games, but you did all the time. I trust you were, Olivia. They took you to that cornfield and left you out there to try to find your way back. I was watching the whole time. Little did they know that the field was festering with poisonous snakes. I got there to you just in time before a black snake was close to putting his venom in you, Olivia. That was a close call. There was no bird's nest out there, just a den of snakes, and those boys knew no bird's nest was there, and they thought they were pulling a joke on you, but what they were actually doing was putting your life in harm's way." "I remember that Jeremiah, the way you picked that snake up by its tail and flung it, you looked like a superhero." "When I read the description of that snake, if it had bitten you, you would've died in a matter of minutes," Jeremiah continued. "I was very angry with them because they knew you were naïve and easily persuaded because of your trusting heart. I was so furious that I almost forgot the path back to school, but we made it back just in time when the recess bell rang for us to return to class. Even after that episode, you still allowed Bossk and his gang to manipulate you into some dangerous places. I didn't know if you would ever learn. It was as if you wanted to be liked by everybody, even though they would do things to hurt you. No matter where you are, everybody is not going to always like you. You will always find one, two, or even a few who don't like you just because of who you are. You don't have to do anything but show up, and there will be some in the crowd who don't like you just because." "Jeremiah, you are giving one of your sermons now," Olivia said. "You, Olivia, couldn't see that, and I guess that's why I love you so much. Your heart is like gold." Jeremiah grabbed her hand, kissed it, and looked into her eyes. "Like the time you followed Bossk and the gang around the corner of the school, and there was Porchia, who you thought was your friend, and she had them hold your hands and feet while she punched you all because you won the first-place trophy for your book report on Alaska. I knew Porchia was jealous of you because she always had a way of being sarcastic about something you said or had done or something you would wear.

Remember when we had that big open house assembly, and it was our time to sing for the parents and teachers?" "Yeah, I loved to sing," Olivia said while she sipped more water. "Yes, I know you loved to sing, but on that particular day, you didn't get a chance to sing because Bossk and Danny locked you in the choir room. I was wondering what happened to you, but I saw your father and mother earlier that day, so I thought they had taken you home. Once again, you let them lure you somewhere, and they fooled you. When I got home, and my parents told me you were missing, I knew that Bossk and Danny had something to do with it." "Yeah, I was in the music room all night. It was spooky, too; the school made a lot of noise when no one was there; it seemed like spirits were lurking in the halls. I hid under Mrs. Tatum's desk and fell asleep. I remember being hungry, but that was a lesson in itself," Olivia said. "I knew you were a tough assignment when I first held you in my arms when you were a baby," Jeremiah looked as if he had let some big secret slip out. "Assignment? Baby? What do you mean, Jeremiah?" Olivia said in a very soft, sleepy tone. Jeremiah hurriedly corrected his statement and said, "Well, it felt like you were an assignment to me, someone I should take care of." Jeremiah sighed in relief that she hadn't asked him about holding her in his arms when she was a baby. "You will find out soon enough what I really mean," he mumbled under his breath. "You were my hero, Jeremiah," she said as she touched his hand. Her hands were feeble and cold to the touch. "I remember when we were on that field trip to the zoo." "Oh yeah, I do, too. We were in an area with a pond and a beautiful waterfall. I don't know how I ended up over there by the rocks." Jeremiah said, "I do. You were following behind Lenny Maxwell, for what I don't know." Olivia continued, "I slipped and fell in the water. I couldn't swim, and I knew I was going to drown. It seemed like what was a beautiful waterfall turned into a monstrous water gulf. I could feel myself drowning, and I heard a voice saying, "Grab my hand." I thought it was Lenny Maxwell, but it was you." "Yeah, I remember the look of disappointment on your face when you saw that it was me and not Lenny." "Lenny was a wimp and went off scared and screaming like a little girl. I was glad it was you, Jeremiah," Olivia said in a stronger tone. "I don't know where you get that from." Jeremiah said, "Well, let's just say I can read your feelings." "Well, maybe at the time, I thought it was Lenny because he was right next to me when I fell," she said, explaining her look. "Okay, Olivia, if you say so, I will go along with that," Jeremiah said. "Do you remember when we had that big science project in the 3rd grade, studying the planets and the solar system?" "Oh yes," Olivia said, clapping her hands. "I enjoyed that project. You and I seemed to always end up on the same team whenever there were projects. It didn't matter if we were sitting next to each other or as far apart; for some reason, all our teachers would put us on the same team." "You can say it was divine intervention for your sake," Jeremiah said as he chuckled. "Whatever do you mean, Mr. Blue Eyes?" Olivia said, with an attitude. "Look at you; even now, you have an attitude, and all I've ever done was try to help you, Missy," Jeremiah said as he rubbed his nose against hers. They both began to laugh. They would always play with each other in this way. "We are still young at heart, aren't we, Jeremiah?"

Olivia asked. "Yes, we are," Jeremiah said as he kissed her forehead. "I got a lot of nerves trying to have an attitude at age 100," Olivia said as she pulled herself up on the bed. "Well, that is to be expected, no matter your age. There is one thing I can say for you, Olivia, which is that as nice as you are, you can get attitude, especially when someone makes you mad. You are the total opposite of yourself when you're mad. You can go from being the sweetest, nicest person to being fireball mad. Working on that science project with you taught me that." "Well, it takes a lot to get me to that point, and someone had to have done something for me to be mad; you can take that to the bank with interest," Olivia said, shaking her head. "And as far as that science project, everything was going fine. We decided to make a galaxy of the planets with the Styrofoam balls, and everyone had the planet they were to paint. I had Earth and Jupiter, and Lisa Simmons knew that we had listed those two planets by my name, and she went and painted her balls for Earth and Jupiter when she had Uranus and Pluto. Uhh, I'm getting mad all over again just thinking and talking about it!" The monitors in the room started beeping faster. "Calm down, Olivia; that was years ago; the way you are speaking of it makes it seem like it just happened yesterday," Jeremiah said as he touched her shoulder. "I know, I'm having a flashback, and just because of that, every woman I met after that with red hair made me angry, with the exception of Victorious." "Yes, I know, and it took you a long time to accept Victorious into the group because she had red hair." "Yeah, I learned from that. You can't put everybody in the same box because of whatever similarities they may possess with a past bad experience you've had." "That is right, my dear." Jeremiah always called her by that name whenever she said something profound or showed any internal revelation. "You really had an issue back then." Olivia said, "Yes, I did, but don't you remember how Lisa was so conniving throughout the whole time we were working on the planetarium? It seemed as if everything I said and the suggestions I made were made light of by her, as she wanted to do the opposite. Sometimes, I swear, I wanted to strangle her, but I just didn't have enough callousness in me to do so." "I know, dear, you've always been the victim and had certain people, for some reason or another, target you." "Jeremiah, why is that?" She asked like a little girl, inquisitive of a father's answer. "It is because you are special," he said. "When you have an anointing in your life and when you have been set apart for something special and extraordinary, people can't accept your exceptional qualities. And so, they target you because you are different and special." "But I've never felt special; I'm just trying to live like everyone else," she said. "Well, I don't know why I'm even going over this; here I am 100 years old; what does it matter now?" "Oh, I beg to differ with you; I think this is a fine time to reflect on your life and how things have been," Jeremiah said as he walked over to the window. "Why do you say that?" "Because you can look back on your life and see what God has done for you and all the great and brand new mercies He has supplied you day in and day out," Jeremiah said. "Oh, yes, I know for sure that it was God who has been there for me. And I believe He sends His angels to watch over us too, don't you, Jeremiah?" He turned and smiled and said, "Yes, indeed, He does, in more ways than you know." As he smiled and stood there, a bright light encompassed him, but Olivia didn't notice because she was feeble and tired. "I want you to rest now," he said. "Don't leave me, Jeremiah," she said sluggishly, slurred, and sleepy. "No, I won't leave you. I'll be right here, sitting in this chair, waiting for the rest to come in." "What rest?" She said as she drifted off. "You'll see, my dear," Jeremiah said as he held her hand.

CHAPTER II

Meet Ezekiel "The Beginning of Divine Intervention."

After about 30 minutes had gone by, there was a knock on the door. In came a big, husky, bearded man. He had a deep voice that he couldn't whisper. In his deep, whispering voice, he hunched Jeremiah and asked, "How's she doing, Doc?" This definitely woke Jeremiah up out of his nap, and Olivia said right away, "She's doing just fine with your no whispering self; come over here and give me a hug, you big old lug," as she laughed and coughed at the same time. "Well, I know you are doing fine in your spirits; you could always be down physically, but it never bothered your sense of humor or spirit. Olivia, that's what I love about you, girl. You are always up in your spirit; I call that a sweet spirit," Ezekiel said in his deeper voice. "No matter how bleak it looks, you will find the positive in it all." "Of course, I will. God has been too good to be all dismal and down for what you are living, and thank God for that," Olivia said in her soprano voice. Jeremiah said, "Well, we got the bass and soprano sections here; all we need is a couple of altos, and we can sing." "Hush, Jeremiah," Olivia continued. "As old as I am, I thank God that I know who I am, and I remember you old farts," laughing and coughing at the same time. "Careful now, little lady; you don't want to cause any problems with your health," said Jeremiah with a look of concern. Olivia looked at Ezekiel and said, "Look here; we have the daddy of the bunch, always sheltering and showing concern, trying to be all serious." "Well, you know, that is just how Jeremiah is and has always been. You can't blame him because we used to always get into something, and here he would come to get us out of trouble, straighten everything up, and clean up all of our messes," Ezekiel said as he gently shoved Jeremiah on the shoulder. "Yes, and boy, did we get into some messes?!" "Yes, you did," said Jeremiah. "You kept me busy all the time trying to take care of you two, always going about experimenting with the most outlandish things. It wasn't just kids' stuff; it would be crazy stuff that could get you killed or cause a major disaster, not only for the two of you but for everybody," said Jeremiah as he looked up and sighed. "Well, actually, it was me trying to just be there with Olivia," Ezekiel said. "I was just trying to make sure she wouldn't be by herself and all, and then I would end up in trouble along with her." "Zeke, I can't believe you said that. I wasn't the one always doing stuff; you had a good hand in a lot of the things we got into. I may have come up with the ideas, but you sure had your thoughts to go along with them." "What?" Ezekiel said, surprised and loudly, causing Merle, the charge nurse, to come in and say, "Quiet, please; you all are disturbing the entire floor." "See Zeke, there you go, getting me in trouble with the nurse and the hospital," Olivia said, whispering and pointing at him. "I'm too old to get kicked out of the hospital because of you and that deep, loud voice. Tell him Jeremiah," Olivia said as she covered herself with more covers. "It's cold in here; I can imagine what it's like outside, and you're trying to get me kicked out of the hospital. I just got here, and you are already accusing me of doing something." Ezekiel said, "Olivia, if you get kicked out of the hospital, it would be because you are a bad patient." "I'm no bad patient; you take that back, Zeke." "Alright, alright, you two," Jeremiah said. "It's like I'm dealing with children in here, and both of you are as old as Abraham, and you act like you are four and five years old. Goodness, you two haven't been together for a good ten minutes, and here we go." "Jeremiah, you should be used to that; you know how me and Zeke are, and we love each other to death." "That's right, nobody better not mess with my Livie, or they will have to come through me." Ezekiel stood and stretched his chest out, and it swelled up like a big balloon. "You still got it, Zeke, don't you?" Olivia said, smiling. "I remember when you first did that when Puncho was messing with me." "Oh yeah, that Puncho was something else; he had a knack of picking on people." "What was his real name?" Jeremiah asked. "I don't know his real name; everybody called him Puncho, and that's all I can remember," Ezekiel said. "Now, it's bad when nobody knows your name but your nickname, and boy, we can put a name on somebody." "Oh yeah, like Binkie," Ezekiel said, laughing. "Yeah, I remember Binkie; he looked like a Binkie too." They all laughed together. "Shush," Olivia said. "Y'all are going to have to pack my bags because they are sure going to kick me out." "But no, do you remember Clamp? Now, why would somebody get a nickname like Clamp? Did he clamp on to something, or was something clamped on to him?" Ezekiel slapped Jeremiah's hand as he leaned back in the chair, trying to muffle his laugh with his hand. Olivia said, "Yeah, I remember that, but do you remember Chicken Girl?" "Oh yeah," said Jeremiah. "You know that one there is from Lucille being out at the farm, and those chickens were flying all around her, and she got scared. Ever since then, she has been called Chicken Girl. Now I remember Stanka." "Oh yeah, and she was a pretty girl too," Ezekiel said. "But with a nickname like Stanka, you'd wonder where that one came from." "Yeah," said Olivia, and they laughed and shook their heads. "But Puncho was the only one I can remember that fit his name, because he was always doing something that made you want to punch him." "Alright now," Jeremiah said as he looked at Ezekiel with a correcting eye. "Remember who you are." "Oh, yeah," Ezekiel said. Olivia looked at them both and said, "What does that mean?" Jeremiah looked at her and said, "Ezekiel knows what it means." "Yeah, but I want to know what you mean." "Never mind, Olivia," Jeremiah said with his fathering voice and his gentle touch as he rubbed her forehead. "You need to rest." Olivia kindly obeyed Jeremiah's demand and turned her head to the wall to go to sleep.

After a while, the nurse, Meryl, came in to check Olivia's vitals. "How are you guys doing?" She asked. Jeremiah and Ezekiel answered in unison, "We're good." Ezekiel asked her, "How is my Livie?" Meryl said she was getting ready for her moment. Jeremiah said, "Shush, she will hear you. She already knows; I've prepared her already. While she was asleep," Meryl said. "You know best," Jeremiah replied with deep respect. "Yes, I always prepare my precious lambs before it is their time. Sometimes they recognize it, and sometimes they are so busy with their lives that they don't realize that their moment is upon them," Meryl spoke softly. "She's ready for her journey, but let us keep her at ease until the time she says she checks her blood pressure." "We understand and obey," Ezekiel said as he bowed his head to humble himself. Olivia was so drugged with the medicines that she didn't budge throughout the time Meryl was working with her. At this time, the patient care assistant named Emanuel, who always assisted Meryl with her patients, came in. As he entered, both Jeremiah and Ezekiel bowed down. He spoke to them and said, "Arise, let us be about our father's business." "How long before the others come?" Jeremiah asked him with the deepest respect. "They will come at their respective times. The process is one that is not rushed in. Patience, my Jeremiah," Emanuel said as he touched him on the shoulder. Jeremiah felt virtue enter his body as a warm touch from a heating pad. Jeremiah humbled himself and said, "As you wish, your majesty." "I will be back when the time is right, and with my Father, you won't see me again. until then," Emanuel said with a voice of sweet softness, like music to your ears. He smiled the sweetest smile as he left the room.

Ezekiel took his breath, sighed, and said, "Just being in his presence is so amazing." Jeremiah said, "I know. Even in your presence, Meryl is so awesome. I wonder: Do the people know or feel your presence in this hospital?" Jeremiah asked with an inquisitive look on his face. "Sometimes they do, and at other times they ignore me, even when I'm trying to help them. You all take care; the others should be here soon," Meryl said as she left the room. All of a sudden, Olivia said, "I could hear voices talking but couldn't make out all that was being said. What are you two talking about now?" She asked as she turned in the bed and went back to sleep. She was dreaming and tossing in the bed, and Ezekiel touched her with his soft hands. She woke up with a smile as she looked at him. She stated, "I've always loved your touch, Zeke; you've always had a way of calming me when I need to be calmed. What's going on with you?" She said, looking into his eyes.

"I was just remembering that time when you were riding that bike that had no brakes on it. You were coming down that hill so fast, I knew you were going to crash into something, Livie." She looked at Ezekiel and said, "Yeah, I was having fun until I hit that rock, and it caused me to lose my balance on the bike. Jeremiah, you were there, weren't you?" Olivia said as she looked up at the two of them, smiling. "Yes, Livie, I was there. I tried to stop you, but you were your normal, hardheaded self." "What did you say?" Her voice got stronger. "I said that you were hardheaded, Livie, and I am still saying it now because you should be resting and you are talking." Jeremiah always had that fatherly look and voice. Ezekiel came into the conversation and said, "I agree with Jeremiah Livie; you were told not to get on that bike, and had you listened, you would've saved yourself injuries and the 10 stitches in your chin. You were always getting into something." "Oh, who asked you?" Livie said as she smiled at both of them. "I was something to deal with, wasn't I?" They both said "yes" in unison. "Well, you didn't have to answer like that." She rolled her eyes, turned her head, and drifted back off to sleep.

"Whoosh! That was a close call," Ezekiel said with a deep voice. He looked at Jeremiah and said, "This long-term assignment has been adventurous for us, has it not?" Jeremiah looked at him and said, "Yes indeed. I think of all the assignments I've been on, and this one has far been the best for me." Jeremiah said as he looked down on Olivia with deep care, "I wouldn't trade this time; we care for her." "Yeah, me too," Ezekiel said. Jeremiah looked at him and said, "What do you mean? If anything, you didn't care for Olivia; you got in the most trouble with her." "How can you say that I was there with her? That's the best way to take care of someone when you get into the trenches with them." "Yes," said Jeremiah, "but the better part of that is keeping them from getting into the trenches." Ezekiel and Jeremiah carried on like this back and forth with inspirational sayings to counteract each other for a good while until there was a knock on the door.

Meet Hannah - "The Beginning of Divine Intervention."

Enter Hannah, the best friend that Olivia could have. Hannah was athletic; she played ball and ran track in school. She was athletic but still held her ladyly finesse about her. She always dressed "well-polished" from head to toe. The right outfit was a must; the shoes and purse had to be brand names. Olivia and Hannah would hang out at the mall, shop at the outlet stores, and go out and find the finest dining they could, no matter where they were. Olivia sat straight up in the bed and softly shouted, "Hannah, oh my, it is so great to see you! I was wondering when you would get here. In fact, I was just dreaming that you and I were at the Likita's Boutique Outlet shopping, and I had just picked up this handbag, and then I heard your knock." "Hey, my friend," Hannah said in her first and proper way. "My, aren't you looking spiffy today in your cute floral hospital gown?" "I know, girl. They gave me this gown, and instead of being mad about it, I just put it on. I guess there is no need to have my bling bling in the hospital," Olivia sighed. Hannah got out of the chair and flung her bags with her. "Well, you are in luck," Hannah said as she pulled out this designer overnight bag with a beautiful white gown trimmed in sparkling jewels around the neck, sleeves, and bottom. "Oh, my," Olivia said with a big smile. "Please tell me you have some slippers to match the bling." Hannah said, "You know it! Of course, I have matching slippers to go with that." "Of course, and I know it," Olivia said. Hannah started bringing them out of the bag as she passed by Jeremiah and Ezekiel. "Hey, you two," she said as she hit Ezekiel on the leg with the night bag. "Come on, let's get you ready. I have a cute tiara for you too. It's your birthday, and you need to be pretty and have your bling on now, Livie. You know how we always do it," Hannah said as she helped her out of bed. "Let's do it right." "Yeah, we do it right, but I figured, at my age, just doing anything is right!" They both laughed as they went into the restroom.

Merle entered the room and asked Jeremiah and Ezekiel if Hannah had yet come. They both said, "Yes; she's in the bathroom with Livie now." "Okay, we are on the way." "How much longer?" Jeremiah asked Merle. "Well, you know, we have to wait until the others come, and we have to wait for the next generation to come in. Have you talked to Obadiah and Victorious?" Jeremiah answered, "Yes, they are on the way. They are riding together." "What about Aaron and Hosea?" "Well, Aaron said he would be a little late, and Hosea should be on the way as well," Ezekiel said as he looked at his cell phone. "Yeah, I just got a text from both of them saying they would be here shortly." "Okay," said Merle, "Emanuel and I are getting ready as well. It's going to be a great celebration for Olivia. I'll check back on you guys later," Merle whispered and left smiling.

Ezekiel looked at Jeremiah and said, "I've never experienced a passing like this with someone I've guarded for so long. My assignments are usually short-lived. This is the longest I've had." Jeremiah looked at him with maturity and concern and said, "It's going to be even more exciting because it has been this long. Just think about it: We served our dust for a long time. I myself have enjoyed this assignment. One thing I can say is that it has been an eventful one." They both laughed and agreed by shaking their heads and doing a dab.

A scream from the bathroom alarmed both Jeremiah and Ezekiel until they realized that it was Olivia hollering about the slippers that Hannah had brought for her to wear. "No, not Vince Camuto's!" "Yeah, gurl, you know I'm going to do you right on your birthday." "Well, I guess I can be branded down at age 100; there is nothing wrong with that. I guess I can go out in style," Olivia said as she looked closer at the bling on the slippers. Hannah looked at her with amazement that she would say something like that so casually as if it were nothing. So Hannah asked, "Are you ready?" "Yes, girl, I'm ready. I don't know what to expect when the time comes, but I can feel it's close." Hannah looked at her and said, "Well, you won't be going out; you will just be crossing over a threshold." Olivia looked at her and said, "How would you know?" Hannah covered her mouth as if she said something wrong but corrected it by saying, "Well, that's what all the preachers say at funerals and all. You know, walking down the streets of gold and all that they say between the hacking and the spitting." They looked at each other and burst into laughter. Olivia looked at Hannah and asked, "Do you remember Rev. Lee? He would have a good old hum with his and say, "Yeah, yeah, yeah," in a tune that had everybody on their feet." "Oh yeah," she said, "don't forget that little short lady preacher. I've forgotten her name, but she would holler as if something was after her; she would say "Hee" in a high soprano voice. I thought something had stuck her in the butt." They both were laughing so loudly and hard until Jeremiah knocked on the door and said, "Excuse me, but you two are just a tad bit loud for the comforts of a hospital room." "Hush, Jeremiah, that's why they gave me my own private room; they know how I am and how I get when y'all come in." Jeremiah said, "Y'all? You don't get like this until Hannah and Victorious show up. Y'all act like three cackling hens in a barn when you get together." "Wait a minute," Olivia said as she was coughing, "Jeremiah, you sound a little male chauvinistic." With that comment, Ezekiel walked by him, shoved him on the shoulder, and said, "Yeah, remember who you are..." Olivia overheard him and said, "There you go with that comment. Hannah, what are they talking about when they tell each other, "Remember who you are?" Hannah looked at both of them, shook her head, then turned back to Olivia and said, "Gurl, don't pay them any attention. They are just mad because they can't look as cute as you." Then she turned back to them and whispered, "Stop that; y'all know Livie is special, and she can pick up on spiritual things. You are going to spoil everything."

Olivia looked at Hannah as she got back in bed and said, "What are you whispering about over there?" "I'm just telling them to stop cutting up, Livie; that's all." Hannah then looked back at them and rolled her eyes. Olivia, trying to sit up in bed, looked at Hannah, smiled, and said, "I know what that look means." Jeremiah said, "What does it mean, Livie?" "It means you two are already getting on Hannah's last nerve, and she hasn't been here for a good hour yet." She laughed, looked at Hannah, and asked, "Now tell me where all the good buys are now?" Hannah leaned over with excitement and started telling her all about the stores at the Likita's Boutique. "What about the vintage shopping sprees?" "Are you still doing that?" Olivia asked as her eyes got even bigger when Hannah told her about the two vintage stores where she found one called "A Bit of Couture." Olivia said, "Oh my, even that name sounds like fun shopping." The other Hannah said, "It is called "High Cotton," and boy, you can find some brand names there, but the prices are just right. That's at both, and there's another called "Sacks." Olivia interrupted her, "And now I know to find some great things at Sax Fifth

Avenue." Hannah said, "No, it's "Sacks," like a sack of potatoes, but you're right, you can still find some Sax Fifth Avenue buys at a low price." "Oh, how I miss my vintage shopping," Olivia said as her blood pressure and oxygen machine numbers began to go haywire... Hannah immediately said, "Now, don't get yourself all out of whack because you haven't been shopping, Livie." By this time, Mearl had entered and asked if everything was alright. Hannah said, "Yes, we were just talking about shopping, and Olivia got a little excited, that's all." "Okay, I know you are all here to celebrate with Ms. Livie, but don't make her too excited. She has a special day today, and we want her to be good and ready." Hannah looked at Mearl with respect, apologized, and said, "Yes," and bowed her head. Just as Merle left the room, Hannah immediately turned to Olivia and said, "Livie, you need to behave yourself now; you've got me into some big trouble." Olivia looked at her and laughed. "You are the one who started all of this; you came in with the Vince Camuto slippers. I do like them; they are so pretty," she said, looking down at her feet and swinging her legs on the bed. "How much did you pay for these?" She asked. "Never mind how much they cost. Nothing is too good or expensive for a human being like you." Olivia looked at her and said, "A what? There you go, talking some foreign language. You always have a way of saying weird things. I remember when we were in class. We were in the 11th grade at South High, and you would answer the questions in our history class just right, but it was amazing how you knew history, and I never saw you study. It's amazing how you would even have extra knowledge about things not even in the book you didn't study. Tell me, now that I'm an old fart and we are far away from Mrs. Burch's class, I doubt that she is even alive now, so you can tell me, "How did you know history without studying?" "Girl, I didn't need a book; I would just listen to old folks talking and watch the documentary channels on TV. That's how," Hannah responded, looking at both Jeremiah and Ezekiel, raising her brow, and telling them to jump into the conversation and change the subject. Jeremiah looked at Hannah as if to say, "You get yourself out of the conversation." So Hannah turned around and showed Olivia a new watch that she bought for her. She said, "Look, Livie. I bought you this Kate Spade watch." "No, you didn't. Hannah, you are so thoughtful, but what would I need with a watch when my time is nearly here?" Hannah said to distract her, "Livie, how do you know your time is here? You never know how long you have." Olivia looked at her and said unknowingly, "I feel it because all of you are coming to celebrate me. I just know something is different about this time. I know we usually get together, but it feels different this time." Obadiah came in.

CHAPTER IV

Meet Obadiah - "The Beginning of Divine Intervention."

Obadiah had a very gentle spirit. He was somewhat quiet most of the time, but when he did speak, everyone listened because he would always have a good point, so it made as he was on the outside. Many women tried to approach him, but he would decline very gently so that it wouldn't hurt anyone or cause heartbreak. He was a good old soul, as the older people would say. Obadiah came in quietly, but he always smelled really good. That's how Olivia knew he had entered the room. "Don't tell me, don't tell me," she said as she inhaled and smiled. “I know that is Obadiah. At least we know that my sense of smell is still working. Mmmn, mmmn, how I love that smell! Obadiah,” she said as she reached for him to hug her. He leaned over, and she held on to his shirt and jacket. “Oh, how I missed that good smell from you! And I’m still inhaling. There is nothing like a good-smelling man. You smell good, Obadiah.” “Hey, Livie,” he said in his gentle, soft voice. “Yeah, that’s my Obadiah. He smells good, gentle, and loving.” “I miss you, old girl,” he said as he kissed her forehead. “Old girl? I may be an old stove in number, but I’m still cooking on the inside. I still have my right mind. So, until I notice something going on around here, that seems a little strange.” “Oh, you do,” Obadiah said as he sat on the edge of the bed at the foot. “Yeah, it seems like the doctor and the nurse look familiar to me, like they did when I was a little girl. I know that can’t be true because they look like they haven’t aged. If I’m 100 years old today, they ought to be at least 100 and something or dead or something. Obadiah, how is that? I only ask you because you’ve always looked at me like something was wrong when I asked my strange questions. But how could that be?" Obadiah looked at her with a sweet smile and said, "Livie, you just have a good memory, and sometimes that can cause you to remember things that are there but not there." She looked at him and said, "Hmmn, that makes sense; I do have a good memory." Jeremiah came over and interrupted the conversation. "Obadiah, let me talk to you for a minute." Olivia looked at Jeremiah and said, "You always come in and stop our plans. Obadiah was just sharing some information with me to help me, and there you come in, always serious about something." Olivia looked at Hannah and said, "What's going on? Jeremiah looks so serious. Is everything alright?" "Yeah, Livie, you know Jeremiah always has to be the big brother to everybody." "Yeah, he is always checking and making sure we are all okay." Olivia looked at Jeremiah and Obadiah as if she were trying to read their lips to get in on their side conversation. Hannah moved in front of Olivia's gaze to get her mind off what the two of them were saying. "Livie, let me try this new lipstick on you. I heard that this is more of a lipgloss that changes color. It is supposed to look more natural on your lips. Let's try and see." Olivia was trying to peep around her to see if she could get in on the conversation. "Livie," Hannah said. "Wait a minute. Hannah, I think they are talking about me." Hannah looked back at Jeremiah and Obadiah, turned and smiled at Olivia, and said, "Of course they are; you are the special girl for the day. So that's why you shouldn't worry about what they are saying. It could be a surprise, and you are trying to spoil it." Olivia looked at Hannah and said, "Well, I know that there is something going on, and I think it has more to do with my birthday and all. That's okay; I will find out. I just want all of you to know that you can't fool old Livie, 100 years old or not. You can't fool me," she said as she looked at Hannah and rolled her eyes. Hannah looked at her, chuckled, and said, "Yes, you are right; we can never fool you." "That's right," Olivia said as she shook her head, poking her lip as she would often do when she felt that she was right about something. "Livie, you better watch yourself now. Don't get beside yourself at the age you are; you don't want to miss the mark with that attitude." Olivia looked at Hannah with her eyes growing bigger and said, "You know, you're right; I've got one foot on the grave and the other on the edge. I don't want to miss Heaven because of my attitude; I'm too close to Heaven, and I can't turn around. Oh, no, I can't turn around." Just as she finished her statement, Victorious walked in, and she entered with a victorious song as she always did.

SONG

Purge me clean; I want to be whiter than snow. So that one day, I'll be able to walk the streets of gold. Oh, how I want to see the face of the lamb that was slain. To sing the songs of praise for the rest of my days.

Heaven is my home, Heaven is my home

Heaven is my home, Heaven is my home…

I want to live there.

By this time, all the others had begun to join Victorious, making an angelic choir and singing:

I want to live there, where the streets are paved with gold

I want to live there, where we never shall grow old

I want to live there; only the righteous shall get there.

Heaven is my home, Heaven is my home

Heaven is my home, Heaven is my home…

I want to live there.

Victorious turned to Olivia and began to sing to her. The others joined in with her singing:

Don't you want to go? Don't you want to go

Don't you wan to go? Don't you want to go

Don't you want to go? Don't you want to go

Don't you want to go? Don't you want to go.

Go, go, go, go. Go, go, go, go. Ooooh

Olivia looked back at them and sang:

Yes I want to go. Yes I want to go.

Yes I want to go. Yes I want to go.

They all joined in singing together:

Go, go, go, go. Go, go, go, go.

Go, go, go, go. Go, go, go, go.

Go, go, go, go. Go, go, go, go.
Go, go, go, go. Go, go, go, go. Ooooh

When they had finished, there was a burst of applause from the doctors, nurses, and all those on the floor who came into the room to listen to them and enjoy the beautiful harmony. Olivia's doctor, Davis, said, "That sounds sweet to my ears." Emanual, the patient care assistant, said, "Glorious." By this time, Merle, the nurse, was picking them up and putting them down in a shout. All those in the room began to cry and wipe their eyes as Doctor Davis passed out the Kleenex tissues. The room was filled with a sweet fragrance, and a quiet calmness came over the room. At this time, Olivia was crying and saying, in her faintest voice, "I really want to go to Heaven. I really want to meet my Maker; I really want to see Jesus' face, and I pray that He smiles at me." Then Emanual took her hand, looked at her with a smile, and said, "Ms. Olivia, I don't think you have anything to worry about," then he kissed her on the forehead. She felt peace come over her like nothing else. At this time, Victorious started another song, "I'm too close." The doctor, nurse, and patient care assistant left the room to go back to work.

CHAPTER V

Meet Victorious - "The Beginning of Divine Intervention."

Victorious was the only one of Olivia's friends whose name was not biblical. However, her name meant "Victorious life." She would always come around with a song or a message of victory. She loved to sing and could sing her butt off. She would always take a situation, or even a normal conversation, and find a song to sing about what you were talking about. So, as usual, Victorious came in, singing the song that Olivia had just alluded to, "I'm too close." She sang, and the rest just had to join in. And boy, when they did, they alarmed not only Olivia's room but everyone in the hospital on that floor. They heard the harmony and the great singing from Olivia's room. People were stopping by and clapping their hands as the group sang, "I'm too close." Olivia enjoyed Victorious, and she always seemed to sing something that uplifted her spirit.

However, this time, Olivia felt something in herself due to the song title. Olivia sat up in her bed and clapped once they finished singing. She looked at all her friends and said, "I love the song, but for an old lady who is 100 years old today, it brings about a different meaning. Are you guys trying to tell me something?" Victorious said, "Tell you what?" Olivia looked at her and said, "Well, the Bible says that a man has three scores to live and three scores and ten if he is blessed. Well, if I'm not mistaken, that makes that man 70 years old. Well, here I am, 100, and you are singing, "I'm too close to Heaven, and I can't turn around." Are you telling me that I'm about to leave here?"

Victorious looked at her and spoke in her sweet, loving voice, which always brought about a calming spirit. “Livie, you were referring to that song when I walked in, and that is the only reason I started to sing the song. It has nothing to do with your age, although we are here to celebrate your living beyond three and ten. This should bring you much happiness,” Victorious said as she leaned over to kiss Oliva and grabbed her by her frail hands. “You have lived a wonderful life and should be so grateful.” Olivia looked at her and said, “Victorious, I am very grateful. I have had a great life, and the Lord has been mighty good to me. I have nothing to complain about, but I just feel that something is about to happen at this time. All of you are coming to see me, and I’m here in this bed feeling a bit tired but at the same time excited to see you all. Let me look at you, Victorious; you are looking quite like a victory to me. One thing I can say is that whenever victory came around, no matter what was going on in my life, it seemed as if, at the end of it all, I had the victory.” Olivia said as she reached for Victorious hands, “I would say that you are my lucky charm, but I don’t believe in luck or fate; I believe that you are a godsend. When I think about it, all of you have been there for me throughout my life. When I think about it even further, you all seemed to show up in the nick of time whenever I was in a bind. I don't know what bind I'm in now; I'm just getting older. My goodness, I'm 100 years old. Is that a bind? Maybe not." Olivia was thinking to herself as she hugged Victorious. A tear fell from her eye, and she wiped it quickly, hoping no one saw it. "Don't cry, Livie," Victorious said, "only if they are tears of joy." Olivia said, "I'm just so happy to see all of you and how you thought it was not a robbery of your time to come and spend my birthday with me. Of course, you are our favorite." Victorious spoke as she held onto Olivia's hands. She reminisced on how, when she first met Olivia, she was at the Metropolitan Zoo, and Livie was standing near the edge of an exhibit, nearly tripping on a rock, and was about to fall. It was Victorious who grabbed her by her hands to catch her and keep her from falling. As Victorious looked at her hands today, they were still small but had aged, indicating her age and the deuteriation that takes place as we age. She leaned over, kissed Olivia's hands, and said, “Livie, this is how we first met—me grabbing these tiny little hands for a tiny little person.” Olivia laughed and said, “If you hadn’t grabbed my hands that day, I probably wouldn’t be here today. I thank God for you, Vicky.” That’s the nickname she gave her. “You saved me more than once throughout our time as friends.” “And I’ll do it again and again, because that’s how much I love you, Livie.” “Well, you shouldn’t have to save me too many times. I’m an old lady now, and I doubt that I will get into too many predicaments that would need your coming to my rescue unless you can rescue me from these aches and pains I feel now.” Victorious leaned over and rubbed her forehead. “Now that feels good,” Olivia said. “It’s very soothing. You’ve always had a touch of healing in your hands. So tell me what you’ve been up to lately,” Olivia said, and as Victorious began to tell her about the ride to the hospital, Olivia began to fall asleep. As Olivia slept, a good two hours went by, and around that time, Aaron and Hosea arrived to help celebrate her birthday. As they entered the room, Olivia awoke with a smile. She said, "I knew it was time for you two to show up. Always the last, but always in the nick of time."

CHAPTER VI

Meet Aaron - "The Beginning of Divine Intervention."

Aaron and Hosea would always travel together, and anytime they were needed, it seemed as if they would be the last to show up. Aaron was a small, muscular, bearded character with muscles that always seemed to bulge out of his shirts. Hosea was tall and slender with his professor glasses, and if you looked at him, he had a nerdy look about him, and he was smart and as sharp as a whistle. The two seemed to be total opposites, but both were very smart, and their attraction to scientific, mystical, and unheard things brought them together all the time. They would both be so attuned to the mystery of things and trying to figure out the unknown that they both complimented each other with thought and theory. While the others would be concerned with the physical side of things, these two would be figuring out the scientific and mystical sides. They were both an asset to the team taking care of Olivia. She needed them just as much as the others. As they both entered the room, they were engaged in discussing the new medical equipment that the doctors were using. Both were so entuned with the machinery around Olivia that they missed her faint Hello to them. It was Jeremiah who interrupted them to say, "Did you two hear Olivia speaking to you both?" Aaron turned and looked and said in his deep voice, "Hey there, Livie girl, you don't look a day older." She turned to him, smiled, and said, "Hey, muscle man, you still look like Mighty Mouse." Hosea spoke and said, "You look good, Livie." She turned to him and said, "I think you need your glasses fixed, or are those some that you made that give you an imagination beyond what you see?" He laughed and said, "Now, Livie, you know you have always been beautiful to me. You have always had that look of a little girl in my eyes. Ever since I met you, you have been my little girl, so it doesn't matter how old you get; you will always be my little girl." Aaron smiled and said, "I ditto that." She smiled and said, "Yes, I like that too, and you two always bring your little girl her favorite; did you bring me my favorite today?" He said, "Of course, I have your chocolate chip cookies right here, and I found the kind that has pecans in them as well. Don't tell anyone, because you know Hannah will try to take them from you with her mothering style." "Yes, don't tell her where is she?," Olivia whispered. "She's over there with Obadiah. He will keep her occupied enough with all the plans they are making for me. I know you all are not here for nothing. I know something is up now because I have all seven of you here at one time. Anytime I have all of you here with me at one time, I know something is up. So you always tell me what's going on. Tell me, Aaron, what are you guys planning?" He said, "Now, Livie, you always ask me, and you know I can't resist telling you, but on this occasion, I must tell you that I can't tell you what's up because I have a mandate that you be surprised." He said under his breath, "This mandate is from the main guy, and I have to obey his orders." Olivia heard part of what he said and asked, "What was that?" He abruptly told her, "Nothing, dearheart. Just know that we have something special for a very special person on her special birthday." Olivia looked at him and said, "You really are not going to give me the details, are you?" He smiled at her and said, "The surprise is in the details, baby girl, and you are not going to get this one out of me." She kept probing him until he pulled out the bag of chocolate cookies, and she quickly grabbed the bag and started eating them. Aaron looked at Hosea and sighed, "Whooh, I'm glad I had those cookies because she was beginning to get to me." "You always had a soft spot," Hosea said as he shoved him on the shoulders. "All those hard muscles, and you are a marshmallow on the inside." "Nah, I just have a soft spot for old Livie." "I think you've always had a crush on her," Hosea spoke as he placed his hands on her forehead.

Aaron said, "I'm not the only one. I think we all have a soft spot for our Livie." She overheard them and said, "You better have a soft spot for me." They both looked at her and said, in harmony, "We do!"

Aaron just smiled with his Colgate smile, a beautiful specimen to look upon. Livie had always been so keen on Aaron; when he would come into the room, her heart would melt each time. She always found herself close to him, either sitting next to him or standing near him. She loved all her friends, but there was just something special about Aaron. There was a closeness to him that she just couldn't explain. On several occasions, Aaron would take Livie to the movies and buy her popcorn and Skittles. She loved eating the Skittles with the popcorn together because it tasted like kettle corn. Aaron would say, "I could just stop and get you some kettle corn if you like," but Livie would only like it with the Skittles and popcorn together. On one occasion, Livie had eaten just a little too much popcorn and Skittles and became ill at the movies, and the ambulance had to come just to make sure that she was okay. This was when she found out that she had developed sugar, as the old folks used to say, but the medical term is diabetes. After that episode, Aaron promised not to buy her any Skittles but just popcorn. Livie looked at Aaron and said, "You are so beautiful." He smiled and said to her, "So are you, Livie!" She asked him quietly while Hosea left to speak to the others, "How is it that all of you have not changed? You all still look the same—no gray hair, no wrinkles, no ailments. Tell me the truth! Something must be going on with me because the doctor, nurse, and assistant look familiar to me. He looks like the doctor I had when I was a little girl. Aaron, tell me the truth: What is really going on?" Aaron tried his best to resist telling her, and just when it seemed that he was going to say something, Hosea walked over with a camera and said, "It's time to take a picture, Livie. The gang are all here, and we want to make this day special for you, Livie." At that time, they all gathered around her bedside and took a selfie with Livie, and the picture was good.

CHAPTER VII

Meet Hosea - "The Beginning of Divine Intervention."

After taking the picture, Livie grabbed Hosea by the arm and whispered to him, "Tell me the truth. What is really going on?" Hosea, with his tall, slender self, bent over to her and said, "It's your birthday; not just any birthday; it is your 100th birthday. Livie, that is something to celebrate. You know how we do it; we celebrate the major days of your life. Remember when you turned 50 years old? We celebrated at the beach. We rented out that vacation home, and we celebrated. We went to the calabash and went shopping." She hollered out, interrupting him, "Yes, shopping with Livie is your favorite pastime. Oh yeah, you remember that restaurant/dinner theater we went to?" Hosea rolled his eyes and said, "Yes, I remember. Remember the part in the play where the host called you up on stage? He was a short little man, and standing next to you made him even shorter." Livie laughed so hard, remembering this, that she began to cough again. "Take it easy, little lady." Hosea said, "I don't want anyone to blame me for something going wrong on your big day." She laughed, saying, "Hosea, you always got blamed for something going wrong." "Yes, I either stepped on something with my big foot, knocked something over with my lanky arm, or was too tall to walk into a building or space. I guess that's why I have the most brains out of the crew. My brain didn't get in the way." Livie laughed and said, "Yes, you were a little clumsy at times, but you are right, you are the brains of the group. When I think about it, each of you has a specialty that you bring with you. All of you together make up a whole, and it is a lot of joy to have all of you as a part of my life. I thank God for all of you." She then began to cry. Hosea looked and said, "Livie, you are about to start a pool of water up in here. We love you, and that is why we are here. You are someone who, if no one loved you or could get along with you, we knew it wasn't you; it was something within them that wasn't right." "Yeah," Livie said, "I had a few of those kinds of people in my life. I hadn't done a thing to that Shantee girl when we were in the 10th grade. She just could not stand me, no matter how nice I was to her." Hosea looked at her and said, "Livie, whenever someone doesn't like you and you haven't done anything to them, nine times out of ten, they see something in you that they don't have, and they despise you for it or mistreat you. Remember, I always told you that." "Yes, you did, and so did several others. You say it in a nice way." Hosea always paid close attention to Livie. He noticed that she seemed tired and weary. So, he leaned over, kissed her on the forehead, and told her in his soft, kind voice, "Go to sleep, precious lamb," as he would call her occasionally. Livie slept for a good 4 hours, which seemed like a lifetime. She woke up to a great surprise. Her daughter and grandson came in to celebrate her birthday. As they entered, all seven friends spoke and left the room to give them privacy. Olivia was so happy to see them, for it had been a good week since they had visited her last. Her daughter was working out of town and found it hard to have time to visit more than she wanted.

CHAPTER VIII

The Beginning of the END - "The Beginning of Divine Intervention."

A good four hours had passed after Olivia had awakened to find her friends still in a group huddle, talking quietly on the other side of the room. Suddenly, there was a knock on the door.

"Come in," Olivia said as she turned over. In walked her daughter and grandson.

Olivia adopted her daughter when she discovered she could not have children. Olivia's husband, Alphonso, was so bent on having children that he pushed for the adoption of a child. He wanted a boy, but when they saw baby Kish, they fell in love. So, instead of a boy, they adopted Kish Anne. Kish Anne Melinda Hill, well, Kish Anne Melinda Bailey, now that she was married. Her son Marlon Lamont Anthony Bailey was at the ripe age of 8 years old. He was a good but inquisitive little boy, always asking questions and searching for answers. That is because he was special and in a spiritual way. He had the gift of knowledge and wisdom; sometimes, he had even been known to have visions. The medical field calls it a premonition, but the spirit world calls it "the gift." So, Marlon Lamont Anthony saw what others could not. As Kish Anne entered the room, she went directly to her mother's bedside and said, "Momma, how are you feeling today on your birthday?" Kish Anne was always attentive to her mother. She seemed to be the motherly type, caring for Olivia and ensuring she had everything she needed. As she went straight for her mother, Marlon Lamont looked at the seven friends who had just left the room. He noticed something different about them, as he noticed something different, odd, or even special about everyone. He tugged on his mother's coat and said, "Mom?" She said, "What is it, Marlon?" He asked, "Did you see the people who just walked out of Grandma's room?" Kish Anne abruptly said, "Look, Marlon, this is not the time for you and your imagination." "I'm not imagining." Olivia said, "Those were my friends, dearheart. Come give your grandma a big hug." He was looking back at the door and walked over to hug Olivia. "Grandma Livie, what are your friends' names?" Kish Anne interrupted and said, "Hush, Marlon Lamont, your grandmother needs her rest and not exerting a lot of energy to tell you stories." Marlon looked at his mother and said to himself, "Once again, she doesn't see what I see." Kish Anne began to comb Olivia's hair and said, "Look, Momma I brought you something to wear, but you look like someone has already fixed you up." Livie said, "Yes, my friend Hannah." "Mom, you do not talk about your friends again. Who is this Hannah?" Livie began to tell her, and in came Dr. Davis. "Hello," he said, and Kish Anne said, "Who are you?" "I'm Dr. Davis, your mother's physician, and I'm just checking in on her to see if she is comfortable." Kish Anne said,

"Well, I've never met you before." Olivia said, "Kish, honey, he's been my doctor for a long time. He even reminds me of my childhood doctor." Kish Anne then looked and said, "Well, doctor, how is she doing?" "She is doing well; she is ready to go home." Marlon looked at him and saw something special about him, just as he saw the seven friends outside Olivia's door. Dr. Davis looked at Marlon and smiled, and as he did, Marlon saw this great beam of light around him as if he were standing in the sun. Marlon began to ask him, "What is that?" Dr. Davis interrupted him, saying, "You are a smart young man. Why don't you follow me? I want to show you something." Marlon looked and was somewhat afraid, but at the same time, he was curious to find out what he saw in all of Olivia's friends and the doctor. Marlon asked his mother, "May I go with the doctor?" She said, "As long as you don't go far." Dr. Davis said, "We will just be at the nurse's station right outside here." Kish Anne gave an abrupt okay as she was taking care of Olivia.

Dr. Davis began speaking to him as they left the room. The patient care assistant, Emanual, walked in to get some vitals, and Marlon noticed he, too, had a bright beam of light around him. As they walked out the door, Marlon looked back at Emanual, who turned and smiled at him. All seven of Olivia's friends were right outside the door, and Merle, the nurse, was there. They were in a huddle talking. As Dr. Davis grabbed Marlon's hand, he felt the warmth of the sun on his hand. Emanual came out of Olivia's room and joined the huddle. As he entered the circle, the room and atmosphere changed into a white conference room, with 24 people sitting around the white marble table with a candle centerpiece and seven candles lit. Marlon was so afraid that you could hear his heartbeat faster, and Dr. Davis, who then turned into an older-looking man with a white robe, long white hair, and a glow in his face. He told him, "Marlon, don't be afraid." Marlon heard music, and it sounded like a choir full of voices singing a song in a different language, but it sounded majestic. As he looked around the room, everything was pure white, and the seven friends of his grandmother had on long white robes with huge white feathered wings, and their faces had turned to a golden-tan shimmery look. He could tell the difference between them; they looked as they did in the hospital room, but their faces had changed, and their clothes were different. There was a stage with three large chairs, small cherubs, and angel-like beings with six wings. Dr. Davis, Merle, and Emanual went to the stage, which was then elevated up to the skies once they were seated. There was a beautiful blue sky behind the scenes and a beautiful rainbow. This rainbow was vivid, not like the ones that Marlon was used to seeing very faintly, but this one was so vivid that you could really make out all the colors, and it covered the platform around Dr. Davis, Merle, and Emanual. Marlon knew this was something different; these friends, the doctor, nurse, and patient assistant, were not what everyone else could see. Marlon started asking questions like, "Who are you?" and "Where am I?" Jeremiah grabbed Marlon by the hand and said, "What is it that you see?" "I think I see Heaven; is this Heaven?" He asked Jeremiah. Jeremiah said, "You are viewing a scene in Heaven, but you are not in Heaven. You are still on earth in the hospital hallway, but you can see this scene because of your special gifts." Marlon, with his mind so curious, asked Jeremiah, "What is going on?" Jeremiah began to explain to Marlon all that he saw, "These are the 24 elders that you see sitting at the table. They discuss the mission of the angels and who would receive or need Heavenly intervention in their lives." Marlon said, "I've seen people with a light around them, and I've seen people with a dark shadow around them. I've seen this in many people; are they like you?" Jeremiah said, "No, not everyone you see with a light around them is from Heaven." Marlon responded, "Okay, because your light and the lights of Grandma Livie's other friends are brighter and have a sharper look. I knew there was something about you. That's why I was staring at you when you walked out of the hospital room." "Yes, we are called guardians. We are angels that are sent to earth with a specific assignment. The seven of us were assigned to your grandmother." "Do I have guardians assigned to me?" "Yes, you do. You may not know that they are there for you, but they will reveal themselves to you in their own due timeframe," Jeremiah said as he led Marlon to a room that turned into a park that seemed like they were back on earth. "We've never left earth, Marlon; you are still in the hospital outside your grandmother's door. I have just led you to the park and changed the scene for you to understand." Jeremiah looked deep into Marlon's eyes as if he could see his soul. "How can you make it change the scenery?" At this time, Marlon continued to stare at Jeremiah, noticing the change in color in his eyes. "It is called the trajectory movement of the mind and heart," Jeremiah said, pointing to the people. "Only people who have a special gift like you can see it, just as you see the light beam and the dark shadow over people. The light beam is on those walking with God, following His commandments, and believing that God sent His Son Jesus to die on the cross for their redemption. The more they listen to the voice of God and the more they grow spiritually and follow the fruits of the Holy Spirit, the more their light will shine. We call this light "the shining." The dark shadow that you see around other people is called "the darkling."

Those who are not following the commandments of God but listen to other spirits and follow after the ways of darkness have the darkling, which comes from the evil adversary and his impulas."

CHAPTER IX

The Adversary Creatures - "The Beginning of Divine Intervention."

Marlon asked, "What are impulas?" "They are the demonic spirits that the adversary Satan sends to whisper falsehoods and lies to people in their ears and tries to plant evil plots and plans in their hearts and minds against those persons who are carrying the shining and who are believers of Jesus Christ. These impulas walk with people just like we guardians. The one the person listens to is the one who guides them." Marlon said, "I'm confused, or maybe my sight is twisted."

Jeremiah asked, "Why do you say that?" Marlon said, "I don't know." Jeremiah said, "That is why I brought you to this park, so that I might teach you the difference. You see that man over there on the cell phone?" "Yes," Marlon said. "What do you see about him?" "I see that he has a dark shadow around him, but it is faint." Jeremiah said, "Good, Marlon, you see correctly. Why do you think it is faint?" "Maybe because he is listening to an impula and has not done quite what the impula said or is not truly following." Jeremiah said, "Good, you are right. This man is at a crossroads of decisions. He is not sure what move to make as it relates to his family, including his marriage. What else do you see?" "I see a guardian, and I see—is that an impula next to him?" Jeremiah said, "Yes, your vision and gift are stronger than I thought for such an age. How old are you?" "I'm eight years old; soon, I will be nine," Marlon said with a big smile. "Well, again, you are smart and gifted. That is an impula." The impula was a gray, hairy creature with long horns, a long nose like a wolf, and sharp teeth like a lion. His claws were long and had ivory tips for nails like those of an elephant's tusk. This impula was hovering over the man and whispering in his ear. "The guardian is there too," said Marlon, "and the guardian is faint, like transparent, wearing a white robe." The closer the impula got to the man, the darker and more vivid the darkling ring around the man became. Marlon asked Jeremiah, "Is he leaning toward following the impula?" "Yes." "Why won't the guardian stop the impula?" "We are not to interfere with your decision; we can give you guidance, but it is up to the individual who he or she wants to listen to, especially at the crossroads of life. We guide and protect only if you choose to follow the spirit of light. There are so many times we, as guardians, want to step in and defend, but it is up to the individual to pray and ask for our help. Once we get the okay and approval from the elders, we move in and do what we do. Your grandmother always chose the right way to go, which is why we can reveal ourselves to her; she is a child of light. Her goal has been to trust God and live by His commandments. Therefore, we, as her guardians, can talk to her freely. The impulas assigned to her don't even try to deter her anymore because she has passed many tests and has chosen to do the right thing every time. Is she perfect? By no means, but her heart is pure, and she loves her God, and He loves her too! She has had many struggles and situations in her life where we had to step in, but we were given the approval to move on her behalf at all times. She had a mother who prayed for her when she was a baby. God heard that prayer and gave us approval to always be there for Livie." As Jeremiah was speaking, the scenery changed to when Livie was a baby. "Is that my great-grandmother?" Jeremiah said, "Yes. She was a pure soul as well, and she had the gift. That is why your gift is strong, and you are wise for your young age, too." Jeremiah looked at him and touched his forehead. "You have a good noggin, and your spirit is pure as well. guardians love to look after people who have pure hearts and love for God. It makes our job most fulfilling when we can help those who love God. You humans are creatures that have a choice in life. We guardians are assigned to you and must do what we are told by the Almighty. So, choosing God over all things makes you a pure soul, especially when you find it easy to do things God's way and enjoy God's precepts. So many humans choose their own way of thinking and opinion. People, especially in these times, have become more self-absorbed and feel that they know everything. They are more narcissistic these days than ever before. That is why, when we get an assignment to help the humble and the pure, we are glad to do so." As Jeremiah was talking, the scene changed to when the accident occurred, leaving Olivia in the car by herself. Marlon looked in amazement, and then he saw the deer on the ground and seven other deers surrounded. He asked Jeremiah, "Do animals have guardians too?" Jeremiah smiled at him and said, "I knew you were observant; you saw that as well." Marlon said with amazement, "Yes!" Jeremiah grabbed Marlon by the hand, and what seemed to be happening was that they were flying. Jeremiah asked Marlon, "Are you afraid?" He stated, "No, because I know that, as a guardian, you will not cause me any harm." Jeremiah told him to be careful because there are impulas that can transiently look like they are guardians. Marlon said, "That sounds like some people who appear to be your friends, but in the end, they turn out to be your enemies." Jeremiah looked at Marlon and said, "There you go, showing your much maturity and spiritual maturity for such a young age." Marlon said quickly, "My mom thinks that there is something wrong with me, especially when I tell her something and it comes true. How do I do that?" Jeremiah then said to him, "It's because many people don't believe anymore. They are all caught up in the cares of life until they miss the message and don't believe in the gift of prophecy or anything. You are special, Marlon, and all the guardians here await your full response once the truth is revealed." Marlon asked, "When I see people with a dark shadow around them, if that darkness is within a person who is supposed to be a believer, what does it mean?" Jeremiah said again that they could be at a crossroads and need guidance. Marlon said, "What if it's not just a shadow, but they look dark themselves?" Jeremiah said, "You are filled with questions, aren't you?" "My mom tells me to be quiet and go sit down." Jeremiah said, "Again, that is because they are not tuned in to the light and the gift you have." Marlon said, "I tried to tell her that there was a dark shadow over the pastor at the church we joined, but she ignored me. What does it mean when that person's face changes to something evil?"

Jeremiah said, "That means that they work for the evil one, and he is controlling them." Marlon asked, "So then why do I see a lot of these images of people at the church, including the pastor?" "That is your clue to knowing that not everyone dressed in sheep's clothing is a sheep but a goat in disguise." "Wow," Marlon said as he saw a man turn into an impula. Jeremiah asked Marlon, "Did you see that?" Marlon said, "Yes, I did. So now he is an impula?" "Yes, he has given in to the evil one and is now his conduit to do evil in the world." "Then the pastor is an impula?" "Yes, and even though he may have been influenced by the evil one, he is now part of his team." "I must tell my mom because the pastor has been visiting us a lot lately." Jeremiah looked at him and said in a strong voice, "Yes, but you and your mom are protected by the team of God! With Him on your side, there's no impula or demon shadow that can hurt you. Even the devil himself cannot harm you."

CHAPTER X

You Are Protected - "The Beginning of Divine Intervention."

"You are PROTECTED!" He shouted, and as he shouted, the two of them were flying in the air and landing on what seemed to be cloud banks. Marlon was afraid to look because it was fast and quick but at the same time fun. When they landed, they were back in the park. It was then that Marlon noticed a little girl who had an artificial leg with a noticeable limp, and he said to Jeremiah, "Do guardians help heal people?" Jeremiah said, "Yes, we are there for people even when things seem to be a struggle, and when we receive the directions from Heaven, only then do we step in and do miraculous things. Some people miss it because, again, they are caught up in self-observance, give credit to luck or themselves, and miss the move of God in their lives. Whenever you are going through tough times, and you end up on the good side of the rough side of the mountain, it is not luck; it is not the lucky charms or even the things that people put in their pockets, like a rabbit's foot, or a chant of some ritual that brings them out; it is God." "Yes, I know that it is God who helps me at school. I always pray before I take a test or have homework that is really hard." "Is homework hard for you?" Jeremiah asked. "There is no way you are a genuine genius in everything you do. The first thing that makes you a genius is that you look to God to help you." Marlon said, "Yes, I do. That is the only way to come out on top." Jeremiah said, "Again, a lot of wisdom for someone your age." After a while, Marlon noticed a guardian walking with the little girl, and the guardian waved at him and Jeremiah. Marlon waved back. Jeremiah said, "The guardian is named Meta; she takes care of children, especially those with special needs." Marlon said, "Wow, she is beautiful. Are all of you as beautiful as she is? It seems that you have a certain look about you that is different." Jeremiah said, "Yes, we have our specialties, and we are here for each person with special assignments, and we each bring what the individual lacks in their time of need. If you need courage, we can bring a word or even just a whisper to give a person the courage they need to face whatever life brings them. If you need love, we can bring someone to just speak to you at a certain time that gives you that sense of love that you are lacking. If you just need a hand, we are there. God has given us the capability to be whatever you need at the time you need it. That is why we are called guardians." Just as Jeremiah said that, Marlon noticed a flicker of light swarm around the little girl. Marlon looked and said, "What is that?" Jeremiah said, "You don't miss a thing. That is called a lighter, and they assist us in helping when we go to war with spiritual wickedness in higher places in different dimensions and realms." Marlon asked, "Have you ever had to go to war for my grandmother?" Jeremiah answered, "Many times," as he showed Marlon a day when his grandmother was young. "She had to battle asthma, and the demon shadows tried to overtake her and cause her to lose her breath. It was then that the lighters came in and brightened the way. The demon shadows cannot comprehend the light from the lighters. When they shine, they dispel all darkness. So instead of sending a guardian in, because it wasn't our time yet, there were the lighters assigned to her who sent the demon shadows back to the pit of Hell." As Jeremiah spoke, he showed Marlon the scene. The baby Olivia was in her bed, and the devil wanted to take her out early because she was gifted. She was only 6 months old, and he launched his attack on her even as a baby. They came from everywhere—from the vents and through the walls; they were all over the windows and on the ceiling fan; thousands were coming after a baby girl. She began to whimper and tried to breathe as they covered all of her tiny bed. She moved her head from side to side and began to say something that sounded gibberish to others. Jeremiah stated, "Do you know what the little girl was saying?" Marlon said, "It sounds like she's speaking in tongues." "Yes, she is calling for help. She has been gifted since she was 6 months old." She was speaking and turning her head. And as she spoke, one of the demon shadows tried to cover her mouth. Her words were causing some of them to grow spurs that hurt. Marlon looked at Jeremiah and said, "Who is going to help her? Somebody help her." He kept screaming, "She's just a baby. She's just a baby." Marlon grabbed onto Jeremiah and said, "They are going to kill her. She can't breathe." Then, out of nowhere, there were thousands of lighters all over the room, and as they came through the vents and windows, the demon shadows went to screaming this screeching sound as if they were squealing and hollering. They all began covering their eyes because the light from the lighters was dissipating them into thin air. The demon shadows that looked at the lighters in the eye began to burn; they were burning on the inside and had to flee. The lighters lit up the room so brightly, and as they stood around the bedside of baby Olivia, she began to smile and choo just like a happy little child. At that time, Aunt Naomi came in, grabbed baby Olivia, and took her out of the room. Jeremiah looked at Marlon and said, "What are you thinking about?" Marlon thought about the times he felt a warm ray of light in his room, and he asked Jeremiah, "When I feel that warm feeling and when I'm praying, and I feel a warmth of light around me, are those the lighters in my room with me?" Jeremiah said, "Most likely, or it could be your guardian standing close by. No matter who, you are in good hands with either the lighters or the guardians." Marlon said, "Are there other creatures aside from the impulas and demon shadows that we have to face?" Jeremiah said, "Yes, there is one creature that is the worst of them all. When he comes around, we have to get the archangels to come and fight the war for us. The Protector of Archangel Michael is the one that we depend on to fight when we have an outright spiritual war. That is when we are all called to come to the aid of humans. Sometimes, you don't know that we are even there. You are so caught up in your own situations and issues that you cannot tell. Marlon began to look at Jeremiah, and he seemed to remind him of a person he used to see all the time when he was younger." Marlon said, "Hey, you remind me of someone I used to see all the time when I was younger. In fact, you are the man that I used to call my tall friend. My mom would be so scared when I told her that there was a man who was as tall as the room. Was that you?" Jeremiah smiled and said, "Let us get ready to return to the others." Suddenly, they were back in the hall of the hospital, and all the other guardians, Doctor Davis, Nurse Merle, and the assistant Emanual, looked at him. Jeremiah smiled again and said, "I believe he is ready." "Have you shown him all that is to be expected on this journey?" Jeremiah said, "Yes, he is aware of all the creatures and the lighters he will encounter on this journey. I believe he's ready." At this point in time, all of Olivia's friends gathered around Marlon, and they began to tell him stories about how they were there for his grandmother. Marlon looked at them all and wondered: "Is this truly happening? I can see these angels, and no one else can." At that time, one of the nurses approached him and asked if he was alright and who his parents were.

CHAPTER XI

The Grave Creature - "The Beginning of Divine Intervention."

He looked at the lady to see if she noticed all ten angelic beings around him, and he could tell how she walked right through them as if they were ghosts. He knew then that he was the only one who could see them. And then he noticed that he wasn't, for several others were around listening to the conversation, but as the nurse walked by, they too were invisible. They were ghosts, spirits of those who had just passed away. They were waiting for their escorts to take them to their resting place, which is what Hannah whispered to Marlon. They all began to wave at him. One little boy asked him, "Are you going with us?" Marlon looked at him and said, "No, I'm still alive." The little boy looked at him and said, "So are you saying that I'm dead? I don't feel dead; in fact, I feel much better than I did when I came to the hospital." Victorious looked at both of the little boys and said, "Yes, you should feel better because where you are going, you are going to have a lot of fun." The little boy asked, "Will I be able to have ice cream?" Victorious and Hannah smiled and said, "Yes, all the ice cream you would want." At that time, there was this loud, crashing noise that only Marlon and the others could hear. It was one of the souls of the dead who was not going to Heaven. The crashing noise was their souls falling into a deep abyss. Obadiah said to everyone, "There goes another one that did not make it." At that time, Marlon saw a grave creature resembling a dragon with seven horns and seven fangs on each side of his mouth. His eyes were bloodshot red, and his tail was that of a scorpion. He came up from what was an opening in the ground where there was nothing but fire everywhere. Then

Jeremiah told Marlon, "That is the grave one. Never listen to him, for he is the author of all lies." The grave one looked and saw Marlon, then bent down to look at him in the eyes. Marlon didn't flinch, for he was more curious about this creature than fearful. Jeremiah and the others stepped in between the grave one and Marlon. He saw this dragon grab a hold of those perishing souls, and he took them into this pit. As they were falling down into the pit, Marlon heard a lot of weeping and howling coming from the pit and from those that the dragon had grabbed. Marlon stood stiff, grabbed a hold of Jeremiah's cloak, and asked, "Is that Hell?" Jeremiah said softly, "Yes, but you don't ever have to worry about that place because of who you are, your pure heart, and the light that shines within you." After that, all seven friends of Olivia and Dr. Davis—Merle and Emanual—came and said to Marlon, "It is time." This time they were speaking of, troubled Marlon, so he asked, "Time for what?"

CHAPTER XII

Preparing for the Journey - "The Beginning of Divine Intervention."

Jeremiah answered and said, "It is time for your journey into the know." "The know?" Marlon asked, and he seemed even more troubled. Ezekiel, with his hand, grabbed Marlon and said, "Don't be afraid. This is a place where all people who have the light and the gift, like you, must go to find the path they must travel and understand the gift that has been given to them. Once you have been to the know, you come out different. Some come out of the know with a sense of knowledge and understanding where they can be a conduit for others to help them on their path. Others who come out of the know and afterward get consumed by it, end up not being able to be used for good. That is why the passage in the Bible says, "Many are called, but few are chosen." Only the chosen can experience the know and come out useful for building the Kingdom. It is for sure that, at such a young age as you are, you will be among the chosen. You will have your own experience in life where you, too, will have your guardians with you, and you will come out on the winning side because you have been chosen. This doesn't mean that you will not face troubles and challenges; what this means is that because of who you are and your being chosen, you will face many challenges and troubles from the dark, grave one. He will always be on your trail to see if he can change you from being chosen to becoming one of the fallen. Never allow yourself to become one of the fallen. Those who are in this stage of life are people that the grave one uses to attack those who are trying to just live right and make it into Heaven." Marlon looked and said, "So the fallen are people who look like me but did not choose to walk in the path of their gift." Ezekiel looked at Jeremiah and smiled, "I told you he is way beyond his years of understanding." Hannah looked at Marlon and said, "Yes, and his curiosity outweighs his fears." Marlon looked at all of them and said in such a sweet way, "All of you are beautiful!" They smiled, and Jeremiah asked, "Are you ready for your journey, Marlon?" He said, "Will I need to tell my mother I'm going to the know?" Obadiah said, "No, you will be back before she even knows you are gone." "How is that?" Marlon asked. Obadiah said, "The timeframe for where we are going is not set, like the time zone here. What takes years here in this dimension will be like moments in the other. It will seem like a lifetime for you in the know, but here on earth, it will only be minutes apart." Marlon looked and said, "When do we leave?" Jeremiah said, "First, we have to let you know that it's not just one trip; it will be seven trips to the know, and at different times of your grandmother's life, you will see." Hosea said, "Yes, and you will be in the role of your grandmother so that you can experience exactly what she experienced." Marlon said, "Wow, will I look like her? I don't know if I want to be a lady; I never would want to be one. I see how hard things are for my mother." Victorious picked him up and said, "Yes, you will be your grandmother, but remember, this is a spiritual journey, and there are no genders in the spirit world. You will be a spirit experiencing a natural environment, but it will be more spiritual." Aaron came by and told him, "Be aware that although things may seem real physically, they are not to harm you because you are there but not there. This is where your faith level will have to be tough, and you always have to remember the Scripture: God has not given us the spirit of fear. Repeat that." Marlon began to repeat it. Hosea told him, "You have to repeat it seven times. Whenever you are in what seems to be a dark place, remember that Scripture and quote it seven times." "Each journey you take will take you deeper into the know," Victorious told him. Ezekiel grabbed him and said, "Watch out for all the creatures Jeremiah has shown you. Do you remember?" Marlon said, "Yes, there are the demon shadows, the impulas, and the grave one." Obadiah said, "Yes, and what are the entities there to help you?" "They are the lighters, the guardians, and... I can't remember." Hosea said, "You will find out soon enough. Now I'm going to give you some gadgets to take with you. Ensure you keep up with them and only use them when you are in deep need or find yourself in trouble. Here is what looks like a magnifying glass, but it really is a light, and when you are in dark places, pull it out. Any evil will disperse from around you." Obadiah said, "That's a great tool to have, but here is another tool: this is a harp. Now, I know you don't play the harp, but anytime you need to have a shield around you, pull out the harp and just play any note, and the harp turns into a shield of protection around you, and no one will be able to see you, especially any of the impulas or demon shadows." Victorious bent down and placed a cap upon his head and said, "All you have to do is start singing, and this cap will become a helmet to protect you from any head blows, or even when the enemy tries to conquer your mind with falsehoods and lies, none will come to you. Only the truth shall you hear when you wear this cap." Hannah gave him a whistle, saying, "Blow this whistle, and thousands of lighters come to your aid. Only the lighters can hear this sound." Ezekiel gave him a can of spray. Marlon asked, "Is this bug spray?" Ezekiel said, "This spray has a scent that dispels evil spirits." Aaron said, "Here, I give you this trumpet. Blow it seven times, and your guardians will come." Lastly, Dr. Davis, Meryl, and Emanuel gave him a peace sign in all chaos and said, "When you feel confused, take the peace sign and repeat: My peace I give to you, says the Lord. Whatever is causing you any anxiety will have to flee." Dr. Davis said, "Jeremiah, I think he's ready." "Are you ready, Marlon?" As Marlon looked at all the gadgets and tried to remember what they were for, Jeremiah said, "Off we go," and they began to take off on their journey. Jeremiah's Journey…

www.ingramcontent.com/pod-product-compliance
Lightning Source LLC
Chambersburg PA
CBHW022107050726
47591CB00002B/704

* 9 7 8 1 9 7 0 2 8 3 7 6 1 *